MILDLY UNHINGED
COMPANION GUIDE AND VISUAL THERAPIST

MICHELLE KEITH

SAND
&SAGE
PUBLISHING

To anyone who has held back, you can let it go here. To the beautiful messes, the deep feelers, the over-thinkers, and the ones who keep going even when their world spins sideways.

You're not broken. You're just wildly, wonderfully human.

and lastly, but most importantly:

For Arista —

My daughter, my co-pilot in life adventures, and, my best friend.

May we always make beautiful memories out of life

First Edition

ISBN: 979-8-9990789-0-2

Library of Congress Control Number: 2025913489

Published by Sand & Sage Publishing

www.sandandsagepublishing.com

Cover design by Michelle E. Keith

Interior design by Vellum

Printed in the United States of America

FOREWORD

How to Use This Journal
Or... don't.
Use it as a
conversation starter or a reality check.
That's kind of the point.
This journal doesn't come with a checklist. There's no "right" order.
No pressure to fill every page.
No judgment if you skip around,
scribble sideways,
or -leave a whole section blank.
The Mildly Unhinged Journal is yours
— to use *how* you need,
when you need.
You can pour your heart out
in the middle of
a messy Tuesday.

Or carry it with you to have coffee with a friend, or keep it in your kitchen to fill in while you wait on water to boil.

It's yours. Make it a beautiful, unfiltered, wonderfully created and honest part of yourself.

INTRODUCTION

I wrote this book to give you a break. A break away from the phone, the TV, the chaos. A break away to reconnect, weather it's with yourself or a loved one. You can answer one question a day, or one question a week .

You can hand it to a teen (or tween) who's quieter than you'd like- but thinking more than you know.

You can write in it alone, in silence, like a therapy session on paper.

You can use it with a friend over coffee, or solo at a diner.

You can use it with your son or daughter.

You can laugh, rant, cry, doodle, reflect, and restart as many times as you want.

This space was created for women and teens who are navigating life in all its beautiful, chaotic, exhausting glory. It's a place to pause, process, and just be — in all your messy, brilliant, wildly human glory.

No matter how you decide to use this- know this:

You're not doing it wrong.

You're not too far gone.

You're not alone.

You're just mildly unhinged.

And that's exactly who this was made for.

A huge thank you to my family for tolerating my early mornings of writing, my late nights of painting, and my never ending hours of editing. Without them, this book would not be in your hands. - MK

Read Me First

HOW THIS JOURNAL WILL HELP YOU

THIS JOURNAL WON'T FIX YOU — BECAUSE YOU WERE NEVER BROKEN.

BUT IT WILL HELP YOU SLOW DOWN, REFLECT, AND RECONNECT WITH THE PARTS OF YOURSELF THAT OFTEN GET BURIED UNDER LAUNDRY, EXPECTATIONS, OVERTHINKING, AND NOISE.

IT'S DESIGNED TO HELP YOU:

RELEASE WHAT'S HEAVY — THROUGH PROMPTS THAT LET YOU VENT, PROCESS, AND CLEAR MENTAL CLUTTER

REFLECT WITH HONESTY — SO YOU CAN STOP PRETENDING AND START UNDERSTANDING WHAT YOU REALLY FEEL

RECONNECT WITH YOUR IDENTITY — NOT JUST YOUR ROLES OR RESPONSIBILITIES, BUT YOU AS A PERSON

STRENGTHEN COMMUNICATION — WHETHER IT'S STARTING MEANINGFUL CONVERSATIONS WITH YOUR TEEN, OR LEARNING TO SPEAK MORE KINDLY TO YOURSELF

CREATE SPACE FOR GROWTH — EMOTIONALLY, SPIRITUALLY, AND CREATIVELY, AT YOUR OWN PACE

FEEL LESS ALONE — BECAUSE EVERY PAGE REMINDS YOU: SOMEONE ELSE GETS IT , TOO

THIS JOURNAL MEETS YOU RIGHT WHERE YOU ARE... AND HELPS YOU GROW FROM THERE.

What Now? Now What?

Before You Begin...Take a deep breath.

Let go of the need to say it perfectly.

You don't need perfect grammar, beautiful handwriting, or deep revelations. You just need to show up.

These next pages are here for you — to listen, to hold space, to meet you where you are.

Whether you begin with laughter, tears, or silence, **just begin**.

Whether you're writing alone or sharing this with someone you love, let the words come freely.

Let this journal be your mirror, your sounding board, your place of quiet rebellion.

You're ready.

Do:

- Write honestly. Even if it's messy, moody, or doesn't make sense yet.
- Skip around. You don't have to go in order. Follow what speaks to you.
- Be imperfect. Spelling errors, coffee stains, half-finished thoughts? All welcome here.

- Use it together. Share it with your teen, your mom, your friend—or don't. Your call.
- Write in short bursts or long rants. There's no wrong length.
- Cry, laugh, and roll your eyes. All emotions are valid (and sometimes necessary).
- Come back later. Some prompts will hit harder than others. That's okay.

DON'T:

- Censor yourself. This space is for your truth—not your polished version of it.
- Wait for the perfect time. Five quiet minutes between loads of laundry is enough.
- Use a fancy pen (unless you want to). Bic or crayon works just fine.
- Worry about grammar. This isn't school. It's self-expression.
- Force it. If you're not feeling a prompt, skip it. Come back. Or don't.
- Compare your pages to anyone else's. No two minds or journeys are the same.

This journal is about connection, reflection, and release—not performance.

Write what you need.

Feel what you feel.

Heal a little.

Laugh a lot.

Repeat as needed.

Don't feel like writing?

Maybe you're not a journal keeper.

Use this book as a conversation starter.

Ask the questions at the dinner table or in the coffee shop.

Use this book as a tool to grow deeper relationships.

An Invitation

And why your voice belongs on these pages.

Before you pick up your pen, take a breath.

This is not another *obligation*.

This is an **invitation**.

We live in a world that's constantly asking for more — more answers, more energy, more perfection.

And in the noise of it all, your inner voice, your quiet questions, your real emotions... they get drowned out.

That's why this journal exists.

It's a place to pause. A place to reconnect with who is inside of you.

A private space to be honest, even if you don't have the right words yet.

Whether you're a woman navigating motherhood, identity, and exhaustion...

Or a teen sorting through emotions, change, and your place in the world...

It's not about being productive.

It's not about being perfect.

It's about being present — with your thoughts, your faith, your growth, and your heart.

Using this journal will help you:

- **Hear** your own voice again
- **Release** what you've been holding inside
- **Build** emotional resilience
- **Connect** more deeply — with yourself or someone else

Some days you might write a paragraph.

Some days you might pour out ten sentences.

Some days, a single word will be enough. Or even just a doodle.

Some days, you may just write a list, or a name.

But every time you open this journal, you are *choosing* to show up.

Not for the world. Not for performance.

But for **you.**

And that choice? It matters *more than you know*.

So go ahead — flip to the page that *calls to you*.

Let your thoughts be messy, raw, wise, funny, emotional, contradictory, or quiet.

There is no wrong way to be here.

There is only your way.

And it's *more than enough*.

WRITE DOWN 7 EVERYDAY THINGS THAT MAKE YOUR HEART FEEL LIGHT—TINY DELIGHTS LIKE THE BREEZE THROUGH YOUR WINDOW OR THE TASTE OF SOMETHING SWEET

Sometimes, the most sacred joys are the ones we nearly overlook—moments so small they whisper rather than shout. A slant of afternoon light across the kitchen floor. The first sip of coffee before the world wakes. These are the threads that quietly stitch our days together. When life feels chaotic or heavy, returning to these gentle anchors can remind us of what is still good, still true, still worth holding close.

Today, let yourself *notice*. Let your soul lean toward joy like a flower toward the sun. Start with seven. And let that be enough.

_____

_____

_____

_____

_____

_____

_____

IF YOU COULD CHANGE ONE THING IN YOUR LIFE RIGHT NOW WHAT WOULD IT BE AND WHY?

We all carry something we wish were different—a habit, a wound, a pattern we keep on repeat. Maybe it's something that started out small but grew roots. Maybe it's something you've learned to live with, even though it quietly eats away at the edges of your joy.

This isn't about guilt. This is about truth.

What's the one thing you would change—not for someone else, not because you "should," *but because your soul is craving it?*

Sit with it. Don't fix it yet. *Just name it.* Because change begins the moment we stop pretending we're fine with what breaks us.

When was the last time you were really happy? Why?

Not the kind of happy you fake in photos. Not the polite smile or the socially acceptable "I'm good."

But the kind that catches you off guard. The kind that feels like **you**, unedited.

Was it loud and electric, or quiet and sacred? Were you alone or surrounded? Were you doing something wildly meaningful, or just... **being**?

We spend so much time chasing happiness that we often forget to remember the moments -

So go back. Rewind. Find the flicker.

Because whatever was true then might just be the thing leading you back to yourself.

WHAT'S UNDERNEATH?

SOME DAYS YOU FEEL GROUNDED.

OTHER DAYS YOU CRY OVER A DROPPED SANDWICH. BOTH ARE VALID.

Is there a knot in your chest you can't quite name?
    A low hum of worry?
    Someone keeps popping into your mind—and you're not sure why?
    Or maybe you're just exhausted from the same old cycle.
    Whatever it is, don't overthink it. Just let it land here.
    This is the space to lay it down, even if it doesn't make sense yet.

No filter required

Dump it all out. Write like no one's going to read it.

Say the thing you've been too polite, too guarded, or too unsure to say out loud.

This page is your permission slip to be unfiltered, unpolished, **unhinged** .

Let the truth come out—beautiful, messy, contradictory.

You don't need to edit yourself here.

You're not too much. You're not too sensitive. You're just real.

What would you write if you didn't have to shrink or shine for anyone?

License To Rage

You're mad. You're beyond mad - you're raging. Better grab a pen because the pencil tip will break. Release and rage.

NEED TO DREAM

*YOU'RE STILL ALLOWED TO WANT BIG THINGS — EVEN WHEN YOUR LIFE FEELS
SMALL OR STRETCHED TOO THIN. FORGET THE LOGISTICS FOR NOW.
DREAM BOLDLY. THIS IS A SAFE PLACE FOR WHAT-IFS.*

So- you want an exotic car? A pet macaw? Or maybe just a shed in the back yard? Or maybe you want something deeper- like true love. Put it out there-right here, right now. Imagine it, dream it, claim it.

LITTLE THINGS

*GRATITUDE DOESN'T MEAN IGNORING THE HARD STUFF. IT MEANS NOTICING
THE BRIGHT SPOTS THAT EXIST ANYWAY.
LOOK FOR THE LITTLE THINGS — THE SMELL OF COFFEE, A GOOD HAIR DAY, A
TEXT FROM SOMEONE WHO GETS IT. THEY COUNT.*

When you start looking for blue cars, you see them. Look for bright spots in your day and see what shows up. This could be as small as a flower blooming from concrete, or a smile from a baby. Seek out the good in everyday and add them here. Come back and visit often.

BEING DELUSIONAL-ISH

Maybe you have a celebrity crush. Maybe you want to be president. Or, go to the moon. This isn't about something realistic, this is about crazy. Be crazy here. Unleash your imagination and be a little delusional-ish.

Surprise memories

THE BRAIN HOLDS ON TO ODD THINGS — LIKE THE WAY
YOUR GRANDMA FOLDED TOWELS OR THAT ONE
PERFECT TUESDAY IN OCTOBER.
LET YOUR MEMORIES SURPRISE YOU. LET THEM GROUND
YOU. LET THEM TEACH YOU SOMETHING YOU DIDN'T
KNOW YOU KNEW.

Think back to a memory, what cones up? Is it last Tuesday at lunch or is it the memory from the zoo when you were five? Maybe it was from when someone was remarkably kind to you? Relive- and revive a memory here.

FIVE MINUTES IN THE PANTRY

LOVING THEM FIERCELY DOESN'T MEAN YOU DON'T
NEED FIVE MINUTES TO BE ALONE IN THE PANTRY.
USE THIS SPACE TO REFLECT, RELEASE, AND REMIND YOURSELF THAT YOU'RE
DOING BETTER THAN YOU THINK.

Life is hard. People, no matter how much you love them- can test you and try your patience. But: you are growing, and learning how to make it all work. Take time for you. Refresh your soul, even if it's for just five minutes in the pantry.

DOODLE DREAMS

*THIS PAGE DOESN'T HAVE TO MEAN ANYTHING. SOMETIMES
FUN IS THE POINT.
DOODLE, DREAM, MAKE LISTS OF RIDICULOUS THINGS.
SHAKE OFF THE SERIOUSNESS AND JUST PLAY.*

When you doodle or create something, it allows you to use a different part of your brain, giving the "other side" a break. Get lost in a doodle, a spiral, or shaded sphere, a lighting bolt or a daisy, have fun. Escape.

NOT THE RIGHT ANSWER, THE REAL ANSWER

THIS ISN'T ABOUT HAVING THE RIGHT ANSWER. IT'S ABOUT HAVING THE REAL ONE.
LET THIS BE YOUR SPACE TO THINK OUT LOUD. THERE'S NO GRADE. NO RIGHT. NO WRONG. JUST YOU, BEING HONEST.

Maybe you hate the new furniture or the idea of moving but you try to go with the flow just to avoid conflict. Maybe you've chosen your battles wisely but something just needs to be said? Host your battles here:

OVERWHELM

*SOMETIMES THE ONLY THING HOLDING YOU TOGETHER IS A
HAIR TIE AND A PRAYER.
USE THIS PAGE TO LET IT ALL OUT. ANGER, OVERWHELM,
UNSPOKEN FRUSTRATION — THEY DON'T GET TO ROT
INSIDE YOU ANYMORE.*

How many times a day do you say "I'm fine." or "It's okay." -when really it's not?
It may be from an unanswered text, or a spiteful "friend" - use this space to rage
it out.

SOUL TALK

FAITH IS NOT ALWAYS ABOUT FIREWORKS. SOMETIMES IT'S
ABOUT BREATHING THROUGH THE SILENCE.
LET YOUR SOUL SPEAK HERE. WHETHER IT'S GRATITUDE,
DOUBT, QUESTIONS, OR AWE — GOD CAN HANDLE ALL
OF IT.

Weather you are a believer or not, use this time and space to seek the stillness of your soul. Close your eyes and listen for the quiet, grasp the peace you have inside of you.

Allow yourself to be called onto the path you belong on.

Overthink here

YOU'RE NOT TOO MUCH, YOU JUST HAVE LOUD THOUGHTS .
OVER ANALYZING? THAT'S OKAY. GO AHEAD AND THINK IT
THROUGH. SOMETIMES CLARITY NEEDS A PAGE TO
STRETCH OUT ON.

Are you obsessively obsessed with something right now? What is it and why? It may be a new show, or a viral snack food- or even overhauling your wardrobe- or something deeper; like deciding to stay or go. Whatever it is: release it here.

LISTEN AND SPEAK

IF TODAY HAD A VOICE, WHAT WOULD IT SAY?
DON'T SKIP PAST THIS MOMENT. WHAT DO YOU
NEED MORE OF? LESS OF? WHAT DO YOU WANT
TO REMEMBER ABOUT RIGHT NOW?

Chances are, there may be a task or situation you're dreading- or worse; avoiding. What is causing that? What is it that is provoking the avoidance? Face it. Head on. Name it. Conquer it.

Reflect grace

*TALK TO YOURSELF THE WAY YOU TALK TO YOUR BEST
FRIEND.
IF YOU WOULDN'T SAY IT TO YOUR BEST FRIEND, DON'T
WRITE IT HERE EITHER. LET THIS PAGE REFLECT GRACE.*

People have a habit of beating up themselves-it could be appearance, , weight or comparison of both. But; what would you say to yourself if you were not you-how would you encourage? Equip? Enlighten?

Be your own best friend here.

BABY STEPS TO BIG THINGS

YOU TIME SHOULDN'T EXPIRE JUST BECAUSE YOUR LAUN-
DRY'S OVERFLOWING, AND THE DISHES AREN'T DONE.
USE THIS SPACE TO RECLAIM YOU TIME EVEN IF IT'S JUST
PLANNING TO SHAVE OR WASH YOUR HAIR.

Self care can be tiny and still significant.It doesn't have to be a Botox session and ten hour spa day. Make time for spa moments. Use the good perfume, dress up for the grocery store. Indulge in the moments. Feel pretty again, because you are a beautiful soul created with a purpose.

BUILDING A LIFE

SOMEWHERE BETWEEN FOLDING TOWELS AND REHEATING
LEFTOVERS, YOU'RE BUILDING A LIFE.
THIS ISN'T SMALL. THIS IS SACRED. HONOR IT HERE.

This season of your life- where ever you're at, weather it's just starting out- or finally figuring it out.... what are some things you love about the life you have now?

Long days and longer emotions

THEY SAY THE DAYS ARE LONG, BUT THEY FORGOT TO
MENTION THE EMOTIONS ARE TOO.
WHAT SURPRISED YOU TODAY? WHAT FRUSTRATED YOU?
WHAT MOMENT MADE IT ALL FEEL WORTH IT?

Was today an emotional roller coaster or was it a lazy river of mundane? Did you feel joy? Heartache? Share. Reflect, grow and heal.

Say anything

*SOMETIMES WHAT WE DON'T SAY IS THE LOUDEST THING IN
THE ROOM.
SAY IT HERE. THE LETTER YOU NEVER SENT. THE BOUNDARY
YOU WISH YOU'D HELD. THE TRUTH YOU NEED TO
LET OUT.*

You never told your crush. You never apologized for that thing. You regret that choice.... release it here. You don't have to use words. Use code. Use initials. Or, write it all out.

Acknowledge it. Face it, release it.

WHO'S FEEDING YOU

*SOMETIMES THE CURE IS CARBS. SOMETIMES IT'S CRYING.
SOMETIMES IT'S BOTH.
WRITE DOWN WHAT FED YOU TODAY — PHYSICALLY,
EMOTIONALLY, SPIRITUALLY.*

Was it a song? or the blueberry scones ? Was it the gym or the sermon? What's the one thing that has happened recently that fed you?

ATTENTION GLUE

THE LITTLE STUFF IS NEVER LITTLE. IT'S THE GLUE.
THANKFULNESS ISN'T ABOUT PERFORMANCE. IT'S ABOUT
PAYING ATTENTION.

Is there someone who you need to acknowledge for a kindness? Even if it was a small gesture from a person you barley know- let them know they are seen and appreciated. This could be a text, a card or a call. Pay attention to someone that comes to mind.

MAKE IT TILL YOU MAKE IT

YOU WERE MADE TO MAKE THINGS

Not just polished, perfect things — but messy, wild, honest things.

Even if it's just scattered thoughts, half-finished ideas, or scribbles that only make sense to you.

That still counts. That still matters.

This space isn't about impressing anyone — it's about expression.

So sketch. Scribble. Doodle. Daydream. Make a list of things you want to learn. Bread baking? The perfect steak? How to knit?

Let the thoughts spill out, even if they're tangled or weird or beautiful in a way only you can understand.

Let this be your safe mess. Your creative chaos. Your beginning place.

THEN AND NOW

YOU ARE NOT WHO YOU WERE A YEAR AGO — AND THAT'S A GOOD THING.

Write about how you're growing and what you're shedding, what you're leaning into and who you are becoming. Even if it's a small change- or a change you want to make. Notate the changes from then and now.

CLOSE WITH CLARITY

YOU MADE IT. NOT PERFECTLY, BUT FULLY.

USE THIS SPACE TO CLOSE THE DAY WITH CLARITY — NOT BECAUSE YOU DID EVERYTHING, BUT BECAUSE YOU SHOWED UP.

Not everyday is a success. Chances are, you got out of bed and that's a start. If today was awful, write about it, if today was mundane- share the boring. If today was joyful -celebrate. What was today?

You've got a blank space...

No prompt. Just you and this blank space, baby.

THINGS I'M HOPING FOR

Hope can feel like a risk.

To want something **deeply**—to *hope* for it—is to admit you don't have it yet. It's vulnerability in motion. It's saying, *"I'm not done."*

Some hopes are loud—chasing wild dreams, finally feeling free. Others are quiet and sacred—peace that lasts more than a moment, a day without pretending, softness that doesn't have to be earned.

Write your hopes down, even the ones that feel impossible. *Especially* the ones that feel impossible.

Because buried underneath the chaos and coping is a version of you still reaching toward the light. Let that part speak.

WHAT DO YOU DREAM OF WHEN NO ONE'S WATCHING—WHEN YOU'RE NOT SHRINKING IT TO SOUND REASONABLE, REALISTIC, OR "RESPONSIBLE"?

Forget goals. Forget five-year plans and what sounds good in a caption.

What do you *actually* want?

Not the **edited version**. Not the one that won't ruffle feathers. The messy, wild, almost-too-much dream. The one that makes your heart race and your stomach twist because it feels both terrifying and electric.

The dream that would change everything.

You don't have to have the "how." Just the honesty.

Write it down. Say it out loud. **Own the thing that keeps showing up in the quiet**. Because maybe—just maybe—it's not a fantasy.

Maybe it's a future waiting for you to finally stop hiding from it.

DOODLE THERAPY

When was the last time you doodled? Was it in Math class yesterday or in college years ago? Use this space to rekindle the joy and entertainment from random doodles. This could be a shaded sphere or a lightning bolt, a flower or a space-ship- let your writing instrument and imagination play on the pages and ignite your creativity. Have fun.

My Secrets

Not everything you carry is meant to be carried forever.

Some secrets grow heavy. Some warp into stories that no longer serve you.

This is a space without judgment. A page that won't flinch.

What truths have you swallowed? What parts of you have been exiled, buried, or blurred to keep others comfortable?

Write the things you don't say out loud. The things you pretend don't matter.

Because sometimes, healing doesn't start with letting go—it starts with letting it out.

PS: You can always destroy this page afterward. I won't tell.

What I want in one year

This isn't a vision board exercise.

This is a reckoning.

Imagine your life in 1 year. What are your goals? To pay down debt? To plant a garden? Go back to school? Begin a business? Start your future here:

FIVE YEARS FAST...

Strip away expectations. Erase the polite answers and polished replies. Five years is a long time that goes by fast. What do you see in your life five years from now?

Ten year dream-ality

What would your days look like if they were yours—really yours?

You're allowed to change. You're allowed to evolve. You're allowed to outgrow versions of yourself you once clung to.

So go ahead. Dream out loud. Dream without edit.

The next decade is listening. Let's dream, and let's be real and let's make them work together. Let's make dreamality.

Travel Goals

List some places you dream to see, and even some places that are a day away or down the street, Write them down, check them off....This isn't about passport stamps or photo ops.

It's about places that call to something in you.

Places that ignite your spirit or heal your soul . Places that remind you how big the world is—and how alive you are in it.

Where would you go if time, money, and permission weren't barriers?

What has stopped you from checking out that coffee shop or restaurant?

Or somewhere bigger?

What would you feel standing there, in a new place, face tilted toward something unknown and new?

Write the list. Make it sacred. These aren't vacation plans—they're part of your becoming.

Personal Goals

This is about **becoming** someone you'd actually enjoy being with when the room goes quiet.

So what do you want to work toward—not because it looks good on paper, but because it **sets your soul on fire**?

A boundary? A body that feels strong? A career that doesn't drain you? A habit that finally makes you proud?

Forget "realistic." Forget "timelines."

Write down what **you want**—and what you're finally done tolerating. Not, things- but habits. Create productive habits.

HIDDEN TRAUMA AND DARK SPACES

What happened to you? What happened that you never spoke of? What haunts you and puts you in a dark place against your will? This may be abuse, or maybe you were the abuser- let it out and let it go here. Begin healing from the haunting of your past.

PEOPLE TO PRAY FOR

Some people you carry quietly. Some you carry heavily.

They may not know it. They may not even deserve it.

But prayer isn't always about fixing or changing. Sometimes it's about releasing—surrendering what you can't control, offering up what **you can't hold anymore.**

Who's hurting? Who's healing? Who's on the edge of something new? Who do you detest? Who do you care so deeply for?

Write their names. Not because you have the answers—

but because you believe love still matters, even when it's invisible.

RECIPES TO TRY

That viral recipe that looks so good and you keep forgetting to google it? Grammy"s peanut butter banana balls? Uncle Milton's meat marinade? Make a list of recipes you want, have or need to get.

WHAT DO YOU WANT TO EXPERIENCE, SAY, FEEL, OR CREATE—BEFORE LIFE, FEAR, OR TIME DECIDES FOR YOU?

This isn't a bucket list. It's a wake-up call.

One day, your body won't move the same. One day, the opportunity will pass. One day, the person you need to say it to might be gone.

So what's still on your heart that hasn't made it to your calendar?

What risks are you still rehearsing but never taking?

What version of you still hasn't lived her full, unapologetic, untamed story?

Write the things you want to do before you can't. This isn't about travel plans or goals. This is about phone calls, sky diving and lunch dates, apologies and things that need to be said-or done.

Not to check boxes—but to live wide awake.

VALIDATION

We *all* want validation. We all want to feel like our opinions matter, our voice counts, and we are *important*. It's easy to feel overlooked and unimportant in today's society. What are ways you can make *someone else* feel important and validated today? Never underestimate the beauty in lifting others up.

A POEM

Forget stanzas. Forget being poetic.

This isn't about impressing anyone—it's about expressing something that's too sacred to say straight.

Write like your heart is whispering to the page.

Write the words that ache to be said.

The things you've never told anyone. The rage. The softness. The sacred. The secret.

This poem isn't for the world. It's for the version of you that still needs to be witnessed.

ONCE UPON A TIME...

We all have origin stories—the ones that shaped us, shook us, scarred us, or sparked us awake.

They don't always start with magic. Sometimes they start with silence. With loss. With rebellion.

What's your once upon a time?

The moment the old you cracked.

The moment you left, stayed, fought, forgave, or fell apart.

Tell it like it matters—because it does.

Prayers and Praise

More often than not, we forget the tiny answered prayers, use this space to keep record of the whispered prayers and quiet answers; come back to it regularly as a reminder that you're heard.

BEAT UP YOUR INNER BULLY

We all have that inner bully- you know the one that points out your new zit or weight gain, the one that tells you you're not enough. That inner critic, who is your own worst enemy.

Step back. Protect yourself from the bully by writing down all of the beautiful, kind, creative, joyful, loving things that YOU ARE.

NOW THAT YOU'VE SPILLED, CRACKED, QUESTIONED, CONFESSED—WHAT'S STILL TRUE? WHAT'S STILL WORTH FIGHTING FOR?

You've written your way through the mess, the magic, the mayhem.

You've told the truth, or at least the part of it you could carry.

So what remains?

What part of you refuses to die quietly?

Name it.

Because healing isn't about fixing everything—it's about finding the part of you that still wants to live, and letting her rise.

LOUD SILENCES

Take a moment here. Take a deep breath. What are you hearing in the silence? Is there a gentle pull to try something new? A prayer for a loved one? A chore that's nagging you? What is loud in your silence? Release it here:

(Not) the end...

This journal may close, but your story doesn't.

One day, you'll look back and see this version of you as the one who didn't quit.

The one who asked better questions. Who screamed, cried, laughed, rewrote the script.

What would you say to her?

What do you hope she never forgets?

Write it here. Seal it with soul.

EVEN AFTER THE STORM, EVEN WHEN IT'S HARD—WHAT DO YOU STILL WANT TO GROW INTO?

You've faced it. Felt it. Maybe even cursed at it.

And yet—here you are.

So what now?

What will you plant with all this self-awareness? What will you water with your pain, tend with your truth, harvest with your hope?

Growth is not always graceful.

But it's always sacred. What is the driving force behind what fuels you? Is it your partner, your kids, your career -or something that you've left untapped for too long?

What have you learned about yourself that you had not known, or maybe simply forgotten before? Is it a love of doodling? Create greeting cards with that. Send out fun notes in the mail to your family and friends. Are you a poet? Create a book. Write poems for people. Are you a wiz at cooking? Feed your friends. Serve at a soup kitchen.

Whatever you have discovered about yourself from these pages; don't leave it here.

Take it, nurture it, and share it with the world.

You were made to create, to inspire and to live fully.

FREE SPACES AND PLACES

Use the following space to write the random things that are popping in your head at the moment. Maybe it's a home improvement list, or a list of gift ideas... here is your space to let it out.

A List of...

ANOTHER LIST OF...

A list of personal goals

HERE LIES MY LIST OF

Notes

NOTES

NOTES

Notes

NOTES

NOTES

ABOUT THE AUTHOR

Michelle Keith is a writer,artist, baker and home school mom, and emotional support human for a small (and loud) army of children and pets. Fueled by cold coffee, whispered prayers, and an endless rotation of snacks, Michelle writes from the heart — about motherhood, identity, grace, and the daily pursuit of showing up even when you're slightly unraveling.

This journal was created as a reflection of that journey: imperfect, meaningful, and deeply personal.

Michelle believes in gentle mornings, messy middles, and late-night breakthroughs — and hopes this journal becomes a soft place for you to land, laugh, and be seen.

mildlyunhinged.org

ALSO BY MICHELLE KEITH

The Art of Gentle Living™

Coming Fall 2025

Mildly Unhinged Living: Being Real When Everyone Else is Performing ™

Coming Winter 2026